THE BATTLE OF BRITAIN

THE BATTLE OF BRITAIN

Essential Library

An Imprint of Abdo Publishing
abdopublishing.com

ESSENTIAL LIBRARY OF
WORLD WAR II

BY TOM STREISSGUTH

CONTENT CONSULTANT

PETER VERMILYEA
WESTERN CONNECTICUT STATE UNIVERSITY

abdopublishing.com

Published by Abdo Publishing, a division of ABDO, PO Box 398166, Minneapolis, Minnesota 55439. Copyright © 2016 by Abdo Consulting Group, Inc. International copyrights reserved in all countries. No part of this book may be reproduced in any form without written permission from the publisher. Essential Library™ is a trademark and logo of Abdo Publishing.

Printed in the United States of America, North Mankato, Minnesota

052015
092015

Cover Photo: Hulton-Deutsch Collection/Corbis
Interior Photos: Hulton-Deutsch Collection/Corbis, 1, 3, 8, 15, 59; AP Images, 6, 13, 20 (left), 20 (right), 21 (right), 22, 25, 27, 35, 36, 39, 42, 46, 51, 53, 55, 69, 73, 77, 78, 80, 83, 95, 96, 98 (top), 99 (left), 99 (right); Bettmann/Corbis, 11, 87; Sergei A. Tkachenko/Shutterstock Images, 19, 21 (left); UK Ministry of Information, 29; US Army, 30; Royal Air Force, 33; Central Press/Getty Images, 44; Corbis, 56; Humphrey Spender/Picture Post/Getty Images, 61; Keystone-France/Gamma-Keystone/Getty Images, 63; US Government, 64; US Office of War Information/AP Images, 66, 98 (bottom); Lebrecht/Lebrecht Music & Arts/Corbis, 71; British Official Photo/AP Images, 74; RAF Official Photographer/IWM/Getty Images, 84; Keystone/Getty Images, 89; US Military, 91; Everett Historical/Shutterstock Images, 92

Editor: Arnold Ringstad
Series Designers: Kelsey Oseid and Maggie Villaume

Library of Congress Control Number: 2015930970

Cataloging-in-Publication Data

Streissguth, Tom.
 The Battle of Britain / Tom Streissguth.
  p. cm. -- (Essential library of World War II)
Includes bibliographical references and index.
ISBN 978-1-62403-790-0
1. Britain, Battle of, Great Britain, 1940--Juvenile literature. 2. World War, 1939-1945--Great Britain--Juvenile literature. I. Title.
940.54--dc23
                              2015930970

CONTENTS

Described as a cargo plane during its development to disguise its true purpose, the He 111 was among the most common German bombers early in World War II.

MIDAIR DUELS

August 16, 1940, dawned sunny and clear over the southern United Kingdom. It was perfect flying weather for the massive fleet of German airplanes headed for London, the nation's capital. Heinkel He 111 bombers and Messerschmitt Bf 109 fighters soared over the coastline. Their pilots and crews prepared to launch a devastating attack from the air. The airborne assault was part of the Battle of Britain.

British radar and ground observers quickly spotted the German aircraft, which were flying toward the Royal Air Force (RAF) airfield at Biggin Hill. The German pilots' orders were to bomb planes, runways, buildings, and any radio or radar equipment they could find. Before reaching Biggin Hill, the large He 111s began releasing their bombs early, over the London suburb of Wimbledon. There were no military installations here, only parks, rows of houses, and a sprawling tennis club.

RAF pilots prepared themselves to take off and defend British skies at a moment's notice.

Alerted by their commander, pilots of the British 601 Squadron scrambled for their fighter planes to defend against the bombing. The squadron was part of the Royal Auxiliary Air Force, a portion of the RAF set up to be used during military emergencies. A group of young aristocrats had founded the squadron. They had money and connections. They drove expensive, fast cars. They played polo and flew private airplanes for fun. Eager to get into the fight, they had volunteered for service at the start of World War II (1939–1945).

Now they were fighting the Luftwaffe, or German air force, alongside regular RAF squadrons. The 601 Squadron included foreigners from distant nations of the British Empire, including Australia, Canada, and New Zealand. Some even came from the United States. One of the newest fliers, a 29-year-old who had logged only 11 combat hours in the air, was Billy Fiske of Brooklyn, New York.[1]

THE MILLIONAIRES' SQUADRON

The 601 Squadron was nicknamed "the Millionaires' Squadron" because of the wealth and social status of many of its members. Only pilots who could control themselves under difficult circumstances were permitted to join. As a test, the volunteers were served alcohol and then carefully watched by the members. Any inappropriate behavior would lead to a rejection. During the Battle of Britain, the squadron suffered heavily. Of the original 20 members, 11 lost their lives in combat.[2]

FROM BOBSLEDS TO HURRICANES

Billy Fiske came from a wealthy family. He joined the US Olympic bobsled team at age 16 and won gold medals in 1928 and 1932. In the 1932 games, as captain of the squad, he proudly carried the American flag in the opening parade. But he also felt right at home in England. He married a wealthy Englishwoman and joined a prestigious social club in London. In August 1939, he traveled to England just before the outbreak of World War II.

Fiske loved all high-speed contests, whether in bobsleds, fast cars, or fast planes. His skills prepared him well for the Hawker Hurricane. Along with the Supermarine Spitfire, it was one of two principal fighter aircraft used by the RAF. Still, he had no training as a military pilot. Nor had he ever seen aerial combat. But he had every intention of joining the RAF, even though he risked a criminal charge of fighting for a foreign power. He was a US citizen, and the United States was still neutral in the war.

By the summer of 1940, many of the nations of Europe had been at war for nearly a year. High above southern England, German and British pilots were locked in frenzied, perilous, high-speed air battles. Inside cramped fighter cockpits, pilots gripped control sticks and stomped on foot-operated rudders while spinning through tight turns and plunging into sudden dives. They all knew the key rule of aerial combat: flying in a straight line for too long with enemy planes nearby could mean death. At more than 300 miles per hour

HURRICANES AND SPITFIRES

The RAF Fighter Command used both Hawker Hurricanes and Supermarine Spitfires, but the Spitfire won most of the attention from pilots, the media, and historians. With its high speed, high-altitude capabilities, and impressive agility, the Spitfire matched up well with the German Bf 109 and proved a deadly opponent for any Luftwaffe bomber.

Nevertheless, the Hurricane was the more numerous aircraft used in the Battle of Britain. Hurricanes outnumbered Spitfires by approximately two to one in the RAF. During the course of the entire war, the Hurricane scored 656 kills against German bombers and fighters, besting the 529 kills achieved by the Spitfire.[3]

(480 kmh), they broke formation to pursue enemy planes. The force of the twists and turns stressed the pilots' bodies. Streams of enemy bullets threatened to shred their planes' wings or detonate their fuel tanks.

FIGHTING IN THE SKY

The commanders of the Luftwaffe were determined to destroy British air power. The German military had already defeated France and occupied much of Europe. Now, the United Kingdom stood alone against Hitler's forces. Germany had drawn up invasion plans, but it knew an invasion would fail if the RAF still had the power to attack German forces from the sky. If the German army were to invade and conquer the United Kingdom as planned, the RAF had to be knocked out, its planes and airfields destroyed. Leaders within the Luftwaffe knew they had to act quickly. An amphibious invasion across the rough waters of the English Channel would be impossible by the fall.

For that reason, Hermann Göring, the Luftwaffe commander, drew up plans for *Unternehmen Adlerangriff*, or "Operation Eagle Attack." This campaign would be a powerful knockout blow, delivered over several days. By mid-August 1940, the Germans were sending huge fleets of He 111 and Junkers Ju 88 bombers,

Surviving crashes in fighter planes was a matter of both luck and skill.

protected by screens of Bf 109 fighters, across the English Channel and the North Sea to attack airfields across the United Kingdom.

Throughout the battle, the RAF was outnumbered. It brought fewer pilots and about half as many planes to the fight as the Luftwaffe. British training schools could not turn out enough new pilots to replace the experienced fliers who were losing their lives defending British cities and military sites. This forced many new pilots into battle before they were prepared. It was common for RAF pilots to lose their planes, and often their lives, on their first combat missions. Others flew several times a day, risking a fiery death every time they took off. Still, with the fate of Europe in the balance, pilots continued enlisting in the RAF.

Aerial combat during the Battle of Britain was very different from the far slower dogfights of World War I (1914–1918). By the time of World War II, military planes were faster, more maneuverable, better armed, and capable of flying to much higher altitudes. They flew in tight formations, and the new technologies of radio and radar aided British pilots in their search for enemy planes. At the height of the battle, in July and August 1940, RAF pilots were ordered up for several sorties a day as wave after wave of German bombers and fighters appeared on the southern horizon. It was an exhausting and dangerous routine, but it was critical in preventing a German invasion. In the summer of 1940, the fate of the United Kingdom relied on a few thousand young pilots.

Winston Churchill, the prime minister of the United Kingdom, led his nation through all but the first several months of war. In an August 1940 speech, he recognized the critical importance of the RAF pilots to the United Kingdom's survival: "Never in the field of human conflict was so much owed by so many to so few."[5]

RAF gunners and pilots underwent ground training using models before taking off in real aircraft.

THE 601 SQUADRON PREPARES

Hopeful recruits could not join the RAF simply by volunteering. Foreigners were banned, unless they came from territories of the British Empire. Fiske had to pass himself off as a Canadian to enlist. Once he was accepted into the

RAF, he was put through a short but intense training course at a flight school in Yatesbury. In April 1940, Fiske was commissioned as a pilot. In July, he joined the 601 Squadron at Tangmere, a frontline airbase near the coast in Sussex.

There were only 20 pilots in the entire squadron.[6] One was William Henry Rhodes-Moorhouse, a young British aristocrat who had earned his pilot's license at the age of 17. He was the son of William Barnard Rhodes-Moorhouse, a courageous World War I pilot who was the first aviator to earn the Victoria Cross, Britain's highest military decoration.

Similar to Fiske, Rhodes-Moorhouse was a top sportsman, earning a place as a ski jumper on the United Kingdom's 1936 Winter Olympic team. After suffering a shoulder injury while practicing, however, Rhodes-Moorhouse never competed in the games. The 601 Squadron welcomed him to the RAF, and by the summer of 1940, Rhodes-Moorhouse was stationed alongside Fiske at Tangmere.

HURRICANES IN COMBAT

Fiske's first operational mission took place on July 20, after only 11 hours of flying time in the Hurricane. On August 13, he flew three sorties, claiming two enemy aircraft damaged and a Junkers 88 shot down. On August 15, he flew three more missions.[7] When he ran out of ammunition, he forced one German pilot to fly into a barrage balloon, a balloon tethered to the ground with metal cables designed to damage enemy planes.

When alerts came from the local commander on the morning of August 16, Fiske rushed to his plane to meet the German onslaught. On his second sortie of the day, Fiske met a squadron of Ju 87 Stukas, the terrifying German dive bombers that specialized in scattering road convoys and killing defenseless civilians. When they dropped their bombs and pulled out of their dives, the lightly armed Stukas were vulnerable. Faster planes, such as the Hurricane, could easily position themselves to destroy the Stukas. On this day, however, one of the enemy Stukas opened up with its machine guns and landed a direct hit on Fiske's Hurricane.

The Hurricane's engine was hit and damaged. Fiske lost control of the wheels and was unable to extend them for landing. He had a decision to make. He could bail out, ditching the plane while trusting his parachute. Or he could try to steer the Hurricane home to Tangmere and risk a landing on the plane's belly with the wheels up.

Fiske believed he still had a chance to land the plane safely. He flew the Hurricane to the Tangmere runway. The plane touched down and skidded along the concrete. A shower of sparks ignited fuel residue along the fuselage. With Fiske still aboard and struggling to keep the plane upright, the Hurricane caught fire. The intense heat reached the cockpit, where it blistered Fiske's hands and feet. As soon as the plane came to a stop, ground crew clambered up the aircraft wings and pulled Fiske out of his harness. They used a fire

BARRAGE BALLOONS

The United Kingdom's helium-filled barrage balloons floated at low altitudes over heavily populated areas. Each balloon was attached to a long cable that a ground operator could raise and lower with a winch. Barrage balloons served as barriers to incoming enemy planes. Low-flying aircraft could be severely damaged or destroyed by the cable. The balloons forced low-flying dive bombers to stay at higher altitudes, which cut down on their accuracy.

The British saw their barrage balloons as essential to the defense of their cities. The RAF set up a Balloon Command under the leadership of Air Marshal Leslie Gossage, and it ordered the rapid production of the balloons once the war began.

extinguisher to put out the flames engulfing his legs and feet. Medical personnel rushed Fiske to Saint Richard's Hospital in Chichester, but he died the next day.

A FINAL DOGFIGHT

At this time, Rhodes-Moorhouse was putting together one of the most impressive aerial combat records in the RAF. Through the first weeks of the Battle of Britain, he scored nine confirmed kills. On September 3, he was awarded the Distinguished Flying Cross at Buckingham Palace, the royal residence in London.

Three days later, Rhodes-Moorhouse took up his fighter to intercept a squadron of Bf 109s. These fast, maneuverable, single-pilot fighters were proving a tough match for the British Hurricanes. The dogfight took place above Tunbridge Wells, approximately 40 miles (64 km) southeast of London. Rhodes-Moorhouse's Hurricane took heavy fire. Veering out of control, the plane went into a vertical dive. Rhodes-Moorhouse was unable to escape and parachute to safety. The aircraft struck the ground at full speed, and he was killed instantly.

The loss of Fiske, Rhodes-Moorhouse, and several squadron veterans hit the surviving members of the 601 Squadron hard. The day after Rhodes-Moorhouse's final dogfight, the squadron was withdrawn from its forward base for rest and recovery. The RAF recruited several new replacement pilots. The continued survival of the United Kingdom still depended on the pilots, both rookies and veterans, of the RAF.

The Bf 109 was among the deadliest opponents of the RAF's Spitfires and Hurricanes.

BRITISH AND GERMAN AIRCRAFT

SPITFIRE (UNITED KINGDOM)

Type	Fighter
Length	29 feet, 11 inches (9.1 m)
Wingspan	36 feet, 10 inches (11.2 m)
Weapons	Eight .303-caliber machine guns
Top Speed	360 miles per hour (580 kmh)
Top Altitude	34,000 feet (10,400 m)

HURRICANE (UNITED KINGDOM)

Type	Fighter
Length	31 feet, 4 inches (9.6 m)
Wingspan	40 feet (12.2 m)
Weapons	Eight .303-caliber machine guns
Top Speed	340 miles per hour (550 kmh)
Top Altitude	35,000 feet (10,700 m)

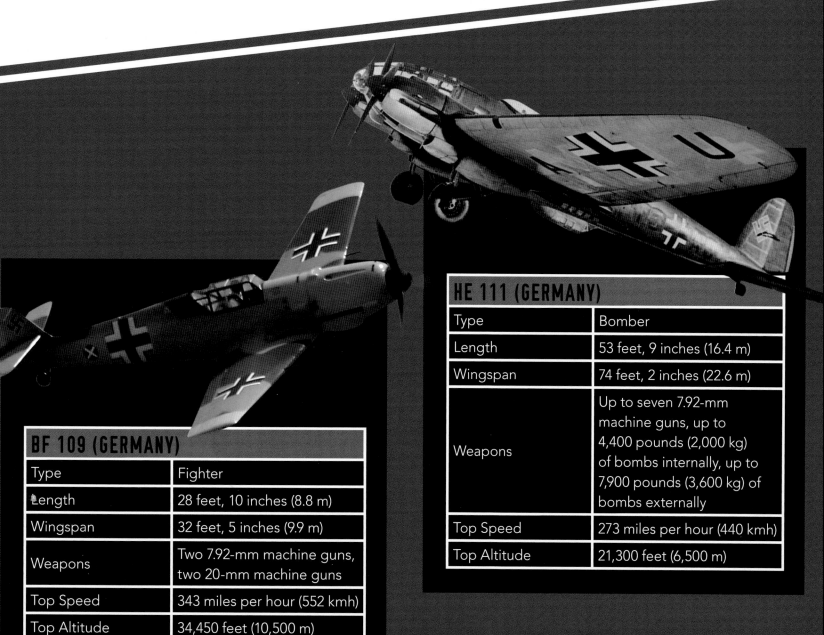

BF 109 (GERMANY)

Type	Fighter
Length	28 feet, 10 inches (8.8 m)
Wingspan	32 feet, 5 inches (9.9 m)
Weapons	Two 7.92-mm machine guns, two 20-mm machine guns
Top Speed	343 miles per hour (552 kmh)
Top Altitude	34,450 feet (10,500 m)

HE 111 (GERMANY)

Type	Bomber
Length	53 feet, 9 inches (16.4 m)
Wingspan	74 feet, 2 inches (22.6 m)
Weapons	Up to seven 7.92-mm machine guns, up to 4,400 pounds (2,000 kg) of bombs internally, up to 7,900 pounds (3,600 kg) of bombs externally
Top Speed	273 miles per hour (440 kmh)
Top Altitude	21,300 feet (6,500 m)

THE PHONY WAR AND DUNKIRK

In the early morning hours of September 1, 1939, the German army marched into Poland. The smaller and lightly equipped Polish army was overrun by the German infantry and more than 2,000 tanks. More than 1,000 Luftwaffe aircraft flew over the border and bombed Polish airfields, quickly wiping out the Polish air force.[1] The Germans also bombed civilian targets to terrorize the population.

Two days later, the United Kingdom and France declared war on Germany. The two nations had signed a treaty to come to Poland's aid in the event of a German attack. But no one was prepared to stop the sudden German invasion. Within a month, Germany had captured the Polish capital of Warsaw and defeated the Polish army.

LEBENSRAUM AND THE VERSAILLES TREATY

German leader Adolf Hitler declared that his purpose was to gain Lebensraum, or living space, for the German people. Germany intended to colonize Poland, forcing native Poles to go into exile or become slaves.

Hitler was a veteran of World War I, in which Germany had fought against the United Kingdom and France. The conflict had ended in 1918 with the defeat of Germany. The Treaty of Versailles, signed by the warring nations to end the conflict, limited Germany to a 100,000-man army, no tanks, and no air force.[2]

In the 1920s, Germany held to the terms of the treaty. But at the same time, young German pilots trained by setting up glider clubs. German factories also built civilian aircraft that could be easily modified later for military use. In 1933, the new government, controlled by Hitler's Nazi Party, established the Luftwaffe. For two years, this military air force remained secret. Germany announced its existence in 1935, publicly defying the terms of the Treaty of Versailles.

Hitler appointed Hermann Göring as the leader of the Luftwaffe. A World War I flying ace, Göring was one of Hitler's top commanders. He received funding, factories, and labor. Göring used these resources to quickly build one of the strongest air forces in Europe.

THE PHONY WAR

Germany divided the conquered territory of Poland with the Soviet Union, with which it had signed a nonaggression treaty just before the war's outbreak. For several months after the fall of Poland, very little fighting took place between the United Kingdom and Germany. Although France had an army larger than

In his books and speeches, Hitler laid out his plans for the conquest of Europe.

Germany's, it failed to mount an attack from Germany's west. Starved for exciting news of battles and invasions, newspapers called this period the "Phony War." In the meantime, the United States remained neutral in the conflict. The US ambassador to the United Kingdom, Joseph Kennedy, urged President Franklin D. Roosevelt to stay out of the war, and he recommended the British seek a peace agreement with Germany.

On the other side of the Atlantic, the British were busily preparing for conflict. Factories were turning out tanks, guns, and military airplanes. British leaders believed air power would be critical in the coming conflict. Bombers would bring mass terror to civilian populations, and British cities would be under constant threat from the Luftwaffe. If the German air force attacked London or

AMBASSADOR JOE

At the outbreak of World War II, the US ambassador to the United Kingdom was Joseph Kennedy, father of future president John F. Kennedy. A strong isolationist, Kennedy believed the United Kingdom was incapable of standing up to Germany. He advised the US government to stay out of the war and deny any requests for help from Winston Churchill. Kennedy frequently clashed with Roosevelt, who wanted to support the United Kingdom.

In September 1940, Roosevelt convinced Congress to strike a deal with the British. The United States would give 50 destroyers to the Royal Navy in exchange for a 99-year lease on bases in Canada and the Caribbean Sea. The United Kingdom used the ships to counter German submarine attacks on merchant shipping. As the German bombing of London and other civilian targets intensified, Kennedy fled to the safety of the English countryside. Scorned by British officials and under pressure from the US Department of State, Kennedy resigned as ambassador in November 1940 and returned home.

any other major city, Britain would respond with attacks on German cities. For that reason, the RAF devoted most of its resources to making bombers.

FIGHTER COMMAND

In 1936, the RAF also established Fighter Command, under the leadership of RAF officer Hugh Dowding. The RAF had a long way to go to bring its fighters up to date. Its fighters had fabric wings, open cockpits, and fixed landing gear that could not retract. With only two machine guns set in front of the pilot, the planes also had limited firepower. They could climb to only 10,000 feet (3,000 m), and they had limited speed and maneuverability.

But new designs were in the works. In a short time, British factories were producing two new modern fighters, the Hawker Hurricane and the Supermarine Spitfire. They were all-metal aircraft with single wings and closed cockpits. Retractable landing gear made their profile more streamlined in the air, allowing them to fly faster and climb higher. Both planes relied on large 12-cylinder Merlin engines manufactured by Rolls Royce. They were armed with eight machine guns placed in the wings, a devastating arsenal in air-to-air combat.

HOME DEFENSE

Under Dowding's direction, the British also built a civil defense network. The system relied on a series of radar installations along the coasts of southern and eastern England. This new technology allowed operators to search for planes in the sky by sending a stream of electric pulses, which bounced off large objects and back to receivers. Information about these echoes could provide the size, speed, and direction of incoming aircraft. The British were the first to set up an

SIR HUGH DOWDING

1882–1970

Hugh Dowding was nicknamed "Stuffy" for his aloof manner. He gained a reputation as a lonely, standoffish widower who had little time or patience for bureaucrats. Instead, Dowding devoted his life to the science of aerial combat. He spent his waking hours striving to create the most effective possible air defense system against the Luftwaffe.

Born in Scotland in 1882, Dowding attended the Royal Military Academy. He went on to serve as a pilot in the Royal Flying Corps during World War I. After the war, he became a vice marshal of the RAF. He was made the leader of Fighter Command in 1936.

Dowding knew air combat would play an important role in future wars, and he worked hard to prepare both the RAF and the British civilian government. He pushed for the military to adopt radio direction finding systems and build a network of observer stations to spot incoming enemy planes. He also led the effort to develop modern fighters, such as the Spitfire and the Hurricane, to take on the rapidly strengthening Luftwaffe.

As the leader of Fighter Command, Dowding was responsible for deploying RAF fighters during the Battle of Britain. But Dowding clashed repeatedly with Churchill as well as other officers and ace pilots, including Sir Douglas Bader. His philosophy of carefully preserving fighter strength, rather than pursuing an all-out air battle with the Luftwaffe, came under fierce criticism.

integrated military radar network, and it was built just in time. They also used a system of ground control, in which officers at headquarters directed the planes to their targets over the radio.

Civil defense authorities also set up a series of observer posts. Civilians assigned to these posts watched the skies for any incoming German aircraft. They used telephones to report sightings to Fighter Command headquarters at Bentley Priory, near London. In cities throughout the United Kingdom, observers were stationed on the tallest rooftops, alongside powerful searchlights and antiaircraft guns.

The British sent an expeditionary ground force to France to defend against a potential German invasion. The RAF sent several squadrons of Hurricanes to France as well. But the RAF forces in France lacked ground control stations and radar facilities. The British pilots on the continent were greatly outnumbered by the Luftwaffe, and there was little coordination with the French air force.

THE OBSERVERS

Britain's technology for locating incoming aircraft, known as radio direction finding (RDF), had one serious drawback. RDF sent radio beams in only one direction—toward the Luftwaffe bases on the European continent. Once German planes arrived over the United Kingdom, they were invisible to coastal radar stations. The solution was the Observer Corps, a group of civilians whose job was to scan the skies and watch for incoming enemy aircraft. Whenever German squadrons flew overhead, the observer counted the aircraft and estimated their altitude. Each observer had a small booklet at hand to help identify the type of aircraft. Observers then used telephones to send the information to the local commander. The system allowed British pilots to get into the air quickly enough to meet the enemy at the right place and altitude.

THE STUKA

Stuka is short for *Sturzkampfflugzeug*, the German word for "dive bomber." The plane's pilots perfected dive-bombing techniques. They would fly high above targets, then dive straight down, releasing their bombs with deadly accuracy. The aircraft were also equipped with four machine guns for self-defense. The pilot controlled two, while a gunner in the plane's back seat fired the other two at enemy fighters attacking from the rear. The Stuka's weakness was its slow speed. Topping out at only 210 miles per hour (335 kmh), it was vulnerable against fast, agile British fighter aircraft.

THE DEFEAT OF FRANCE

In May 1940, the Phony War ended when Germany invaded France. German armies poured across the plains of northern France and Belgium. German tanks rushed westward to the French coast along the English Channel, dividing the British and French armies. From above, He 110 bombers hit cities, railway lines, airfields, and artillery posts. Stuka dive bombers scattered civilian and military convoys along the roads. Armed with machine guns, a single bomb, and a screeching siren that sounded as the plane dove toward the ground, the Stuka was one of Germany's most terrifying and effective weapons early in the war. By late May 1940, the British Expeditionary Force was retreating to the French port of Dunkirk.

The RAF did not want to lose any more planes over France. Fighter Command leader Dowding calculated that 60 full-strength squadrons, each containing 12 planes, would be required for the successful defense of Britain. After losing planes in France in the spring of 1940, the RAF was down to approximately 40 squadrons.[3]

But while German tanks, infantry, and artillery stood poised to attack the cornered forces at Dunkirk, Hitler made a fateful decision. Fearing the German

Observers plotted the courses of incoming German planes.

OPERATION DYNAMO

The evacuation of the British Expeditionary Force from Dunkirk was known as Operation Dynamo. Its planners faced serious problems. Large military ships could only navigate through deep water. But the beach at Dunkirk lay astride a shallow stretch of water where the destroyers and larger transports could not go.

The answer was to enlist a fleet of smaller craft to either ferry the troops to the larger ships farther from the coast or take them all the way across the English Channel. Hundreds of boats took part in the operation. They ranged from fishing vessels to private yachts. The smallest craft to take part in the evacuation was the *Tamzine*, an 18-foot (5.5 m) fishing boat.[4] The *Tamzine* survived the war and later went on display at London's Imperial War Museum.

lines were overextended and vulnerable to a counterattack, Hitler ordered a temporary halt. The British Expeditionary Force took advantage of this time to evacuate from Dunkirk and return to the United Kingdom in preparation for Germany's expected invasion.

Retreating British forces watched as smoke from the German bombardment rose over Dunkirk.

As Nazi Germany rampaged across continental Europe, British pilots prepared to defend their island nation.

CHAPTER
★ **3** ★

THEIR FINEST HOUR

The evacuation of the British from Dunkirk left France alone to face the overwhelming German army. As the French armies crumbled, German bombers cleared the last obstacles on the roads to Paris, the French capital. The French government appealed to Churchill for more British fighters to stave off the German advance.

In stormy meetings with government ministers, Dowding argued against sending any more planes to France. In his opinion, France was finished. He said Britain's valuable Hurricanes and Spitfires—along with their trained pilots—would be sacrificed to a losing cause if they were sent to France. Determined to help the French hold out as long as possible, Churchill was in favor of sending more RAF squadrons across the channel.

Ultimately, as the German advance continued, Dowding's view prevailed. Churchill reluctantly held back further assistance.

French generals declared Paris an open city; the French army would not fight to defend it. The city fell on June 14. Soon afterward, French leaders agreed to an armistice that allowed the occupation of the country by German troops. Hitler insisted on having the agreement signed at Compiègne, in the same railcar in which Germany had signed its armistice papers at the end of World War I in 1918.

There was now very little standing in the way of a German invasion. Hitler believed conquering the United Kingdom was his country's destiny. As long as the British remained a hostile, defiant enemy on his western flank, German dominance of the rest of Europe would be problematic. He knew the issue would be especially serious if he ever went to war with the Soviet Union in the east.

With the British still defiant, Hitler concluded only an invasion would convince them to surrender. On July 16, Hitler ordered the German army and navy to draw up invasion plans under the code name Operation Sea Lion. But without control of the skies, an invasion would be a difficult proposition. Hitler's Luftwaffe commander, Hermann Göring, believed the Luftwaffe could win this battle.

Since the establishment of the Luftwaffe in 1935, Göring had ensured his air force was the best-equipped and most prestigious branch of the German armed forces. German pilots, in contrast to infantry, navy, or tank units, enjoyed comfortable barracks and good pay. They were also given thorough pilot training, and their equipment was in general reliable and well maintained. Luftwaffe victories were given prominent coverage in the media and were used as a weapon in Germany's ongoing propaganda war against the Allies.

Göring, a decorated World War I fighter pilot, became one of Hitler's top deputies.

PREPARING FOR WAR

With the threat of invasion looming, the British prepared. Local Defense Volunteer forces formed in cities and villages throughout the country. They trained in any available open space, building roadblocks and trenches to prepare for a ground war. Road signs were removed to prevent the enemy from easily navigating country lanes and highways. Children were sent out of the cities for their own protection, with some even traveling to safety in Canada and the United States.

Aircraft factories began churning out Hurricanes and Spitfires at a rapid rate. Churchill appointed his friend William Maxwell Aitken, Lord Beaverbrook, as the minister of aircraft. A wealthy newspaper baron, Beaverbrook accepted the post and set to work. His loud, rude, brash manner intimidated employees and sparked furious arguments with government officials. Beaverbrook did not bother with meetings or committees. He simply called Dowding every night and asked the Fighter Command leader how many new planes he needed the next day. He then ordered the factories to deliver them—or else. Air Transport Auxiliary pilots, many of them young women, transported each new fighter to its designated

INTERNMENT

In the spring of 1940, World War II combat began for the British military when the Germans invaded France, Belgium, Luxembourg, and the Netherlands. Following the invasions, the British government took action against people it saw as potentially hostile—those from the enemy nations. The police rounded up Germans and Italians living near the channel coast and sent them to internment camps. These camps were spread all over the United Kingdom. Most of those interned were released by February 1941.

airfield. During the Battle of Britain, the production of fighters nearly doubled, increasing to 500 per month.[1]

In June 1940, German planes began flying over the English Channel, attacking merchant ships carrying coal and other essential supplies. Stukas and Ju 88 bombers sank dozens of ships. Coming in low and fast from French airfields, they evaded the British radar system. British fighters could not scramble in time to intercept the groups of bombers.

The British sector commanders were under strict control from Bentley Priory. Dowding did not allow fighters to operate outside of defined areas. He instructed the commanders to send only a limited number of fighters to meet the bomber attacks in the channel. Their instructions were to avoid fighter-to-fighter combat

"WE SHALL NEVER SURRENDER"

After succeeding Prime Minister Neville Chamberlain in May 1940, Churchill stubbornly refused to negotiate with Hitler. He roused British civilians and soldiers to keep up the war effort despite the brutal Luftwaffe attacks from the air. Churchill gave one of his most famous speeches in Parliament on June 4, 1940. The best-known portion of his speech rang in the minds of British civilians throughout the war:

We shall go on to the end, we shall fight in France, we shall fight on the seas and oceans, we shall fight with growing confidence and growing strength in the air, we shall defend our island, whatever the cost may be, we shall fight on the beaches, we shall fight on the landing grounds, we shall fight in the fields and in the streets, we shall fight in the hills; we shall never surrender, and even if, which I do not for a moment believe, this Island or a large part of it were subjugated and starving, then our Empire beyond the seas, armed and guarded by the British Fleet, would carry on the struggle, until, in God's good time, the New World, with all its power and might, steps forth to the rescue and the liberation of the old.[2]

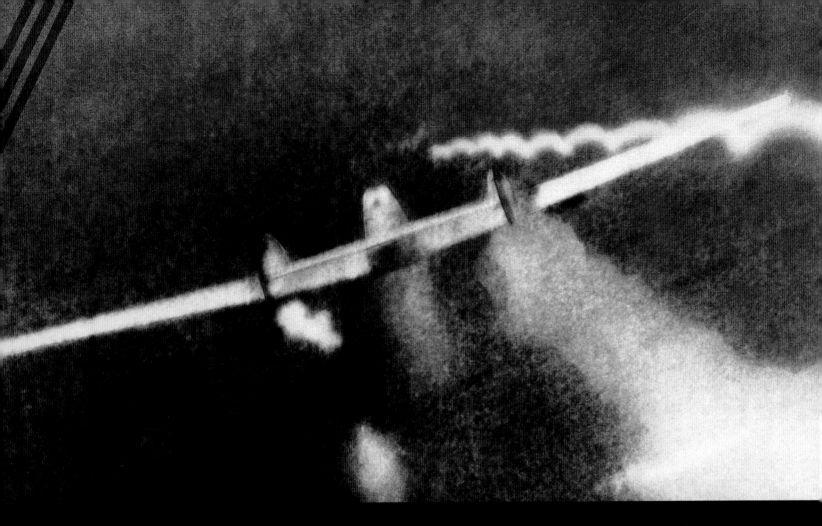

Spitfires with cameras that began recording when the pilot fired his guns captured images of German aircraft being shot down.

wherever possible. Dowding wanted to bluff the Germans into thinking the RAF was much weaker than it really was.

The Luftwaffe took the bait. Confident of their superiority in numbers, they spread their attacks over a wide area, allowing the British fighters to pick off bombers where they could. Downed German pilots and crews who survived became prisoners of the United Kingdom. They were lost to the Luftwaffe for the rest of the war. But RAF pilots who lost their planes could parachute into friendly territory and return to the skies immediately.

SETTING THE STAGE FOR THE BATTLE OF BRITAIN

Hitler was confident the Luftwaffe could handle the RAF and decimate British industry from the air without using ground troops. Believing aerial attacks might force the British to surrender before an invasion could even take place, Hitler postponed Operation Sea Lion until September.

German planes now began appearing in the skies of the United Kingdom, rather than just over the channel. They attacked targets along the southern coast at Dover and other English Channel ports. The low-flying planes dropped bombs on roads, railroads, factories, and airfields. British antiaircraft guns swung into action, filling the skies with deadly bursts of airborne shrapnel known as flak that could take down planes. In the meantime, the RAF trained new pilots at an accelerating pace.

On July 3, Churchill made one of his most difficult decisions of the war. He instructed the Royal Navy to demand the surrender of French ships at a harbor on the Algerian coast. Fearing the Germans would seize the ships and use them against the Allies, the British commanders gave the French six hours to either sail to British ports or sink themselves. In the evening, after the deadline had passed with no sign of action from the ships, the British opened fire, sinking the vessels and killing 1,200 sailors.[3]

The British sinking of the French fleet in Algeria increased tensions between the United

The destruction of the French fleet infuriated Hitler. In the German leader's eyes, Churchill and the British were stubbornly refusing to admit Germany's superior firepower would eventually defeat them. In August, Hitler ordered the Luftwaffe to prepare for a major air campaign to eliminate the British defenses. Plans for Operation Adlerangriff, the climactic assault of the Battle of Britain, went ahead.

SINKING THE FRENCH FLEET

Germany was not the only power enraged by the British sinking of French ships off the coast of Algeria. Vichy France, the country set up as a Nazi puppet state after the German invasion, cut off diplomatic relations with the United Kingdom following the sinking. In 1942, Vichy French sailors at the southern French port of Toulon sank their own ships in order to prevent the Germans from seizing them.

Hitler and Göring sought to destroy the RAF once and for all in a massive, coordinated

EAGLE ATTACK

Göring's orders were to destroy the RAF, starting with Fighter Command. Hitler had reacted to the sinking of the French fleet in Algeria with shock and anger. In his view, Churchill was a madman who would never listen to reason and did not recognize when he was beaten. Only an invasion would settle things. The Luftwaffe began preparing the United Kingdom for the German invasion by bombing RAF facilities.

Göring and his commanders planned the operation in great detail. Every squadron and every plane had a target. Messerschmitt fighters would stick close to the bombers. They were required to stay within sight. Only when Spitfires and Hurricanes approached would they engage the enemy.

German planners believed it would take only a few days of good flying weather to finish the job. German intelligence officials

A FIGHTER PILOT MEETS THE LUFTWAFFE COMMANDER

Luftwaffe ace Gunther Rall saw action during the Battle of Britain and against the Soviet Union. He survived being shot down eight times. However, the pilot did not think much of Luftwaffe commander Hermann Göring:

> At the time I became acquainted with him, I was cold to him. He was a big fat man, a very pompous man, and not only I but my comrades felt that he was out of touch with reality. . . . Hermann Göring would make silly statements to Hitler. Hitler said, "You are the leader of the air force," and [Göring] made a long statement about the Battle of Britain, you know, that he would triumph over the Royal Air Force, which was wrong, as we had tremendous losses in our fighter fleet that we never recovered from during the war.[2]

believed the RAF was down to its last 400 planes, giving Germany a five-to-one advantage.[1]

ADLERANGRIFF

Operation Adlerangriff began on August 13, 1940. In southern England, Heinkel and Junkers bombers struck RAF radar installations and airfields. The next day would be an all-out attack, using every resource the Luftwaffe could bring. Hundreds of planes and pilots were readied for action. The first squadrons left their bases at dawn. But the weather was uncertain. Patchy clouds and fog limited visibility. Early in the morning, Göring sent out an order postponing the assault until the afternoon.

Some of the early pilots turned back. Others pressed ahead. Some German bombers saw their fighter escorts return to base. The escorts that remained lost sight of their bombers in the clouds. Formations broke up, and the Germans managed to hit only a few scattered airfields. All of them belonged to RAF Coastal Command, dedicated to the defense of the British shoreline. Repair crews quickly mended the damage.

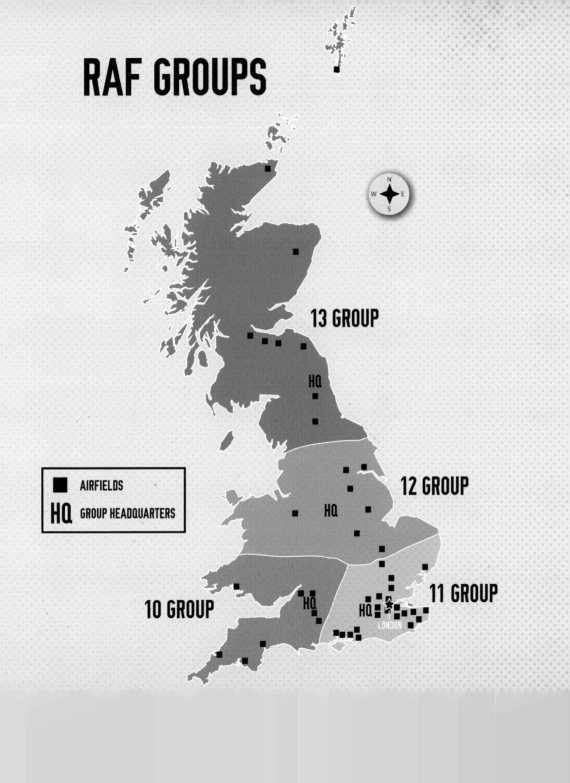

RAF GROUPS

13 GROUP

12 GROUP

11 GROUP

10 GROUP

HQ

■ AIRFIELDS

HQ GROUP HEADQUARTERS

LONDON

The Fighter Command airfields, which housed the majority of RAF fighters, went untouched.

On a mission to strike a Spitfire factory in Southampton, a fleet of 200 Ju 88s reached the city.[3] But their bombs went off course, hitting only a few scattered civilian factories and warehouses. The aircraft plant was untouched. Another raid on the city of Rochester heavily damaged an aircraft factory. But this facility made bombers—not Spitfire or Hurricane fighters.

The Fighter Command ground control system proved effective. From Bentley Priory, information on the incoming German squadrons went out to group commanders, who in turn alerted the individual sectors. Sector commanders were free to send up squadrons at will. Whenever a large formation of German planes crossed the coast, one or two squadrons of British fighters took off to meet them. Facing the fighters and harsh antiaircraft fire from the ground, many German bombers turned back, dropping their bombs into the sea before returning to base.

The Luftwaffe commanders had hoped for a decisive day. But they took heavy losses, while the RAF lost relatively few planes. The German attacks continued. On August 14, the Luftwaffe hit several Fighter Command airfields and rail lines, but repairs were made within hours. On the next day, the Luftwaffe planned to mount the largest assault of the war.

CONTROVERSY

To the British, the successful response during three days of German raids hardly represented a victory. Instead, there seemed to be no end to the planes crossing the coasts of England. On August 15, the Luftwaffe sent more than 1,000 aircraft

British civilians sometimes crowded around to get a look at downed enemy aircraft.

to attack dozens of targets in southern and northern England.[4] Billy Fiske and William Rhodes-Moorhouse were among the many RAF pilots killed in the ensuing air battles.

Not all the British commanders felt satisfied with their nation's response to the German attacks. Trafford Leigh-Mallory, the commander of 12 Group, was unhappy with the supporting role played by his pilots. He believed Keith Park's 11 Group—covering the southeast and London—was getting all the glory.

He also saw Dowding's strategy as timid. Sending up one or two squadrons at a time was doing nothing to stop or even slow down the Luftwaffe. He felt the RAF should instead strike back hard with what he called "big wings"—four or five full squadrons, totaling up to 60 planes at a time. Ace pilot Douglas Bader, one of the top RAF fliers of the Battle of Britain, agreed with Mallory.

Dowding resisted. He believed in sending one or two squadrons to answer the German bomber waves. By doing this, the RAF could keep the majority of its crews rested and ready, maintain more squadrons in reserve, and send up the fighters only when absolutely necessary. There would be less wastage of planes and pilots, and the Germans would be fooled into believing the RAF was weaker than it really was. Dowding also believed "big wings" took too long to form up. Pilots had to circle the airfields idly while the rest of their squadrons took off and got into formation. By the time the big wing was in the air and prepared, the German bombers could cover many miles. In this debate, Dowding prevailed. But his opponents in Fighter Command, and in the Air Ministry, still believed his strategy was obsolete. The dispute would continue throughout the Battle of Britain.

GROUND RULES

Dowding was never happy to hear of British fighters simply attacking a squadron of fighters or following the enemy back over the English Channel. The purpose of the RAF, in Dowding's view, was to keep its planes and pilots intact and shoot down as many bombers as possible. For this reason, Dowding banned all group commanders from scrambling pilots just for the sake of a dogfight. He ordered that no Germans were to be pursued beyond the coast.

SIR DOUGLAS BADER

1910–1982

Sir Douglas Bader was a daredevil and a show-off who took many risks in the air. But he also turned out to be one of the most successful fighter pilots in RAF history. Joining the RAF in 1928 and earning a pilot officer's commission in 1930 did not prevent him from practicing his low-altitude stunts. In December 1931, his luck turned bad at Woodley Airfield. While doing some rolls, his plane's wing caught the ground. The plane crumpled to the earth, crushing the lower half of Bader's body. An emergency surgeon saved his life, but both of his legs were amputated.

It seemed Bader's flying days might be over. He was dismissed from the RAF, but he returned to duty at the outbreak of World War II in 1939. Reluctantly, the recruiting officers allowed Bader to train in the newer fighters using artificial legs. He soon returned to active service.

His artificial legs gave Bader a crucial advantage over other pilots. During dogfighting maneuvers, blood could be forced from pilots' heads into their legs, causing them to black out. But Bader was immune to this problem. He joined 242 Squadron and flew Hawker Hurricanes, scoring his first victories over Dunkirk during the British evacuation. He went on to earn 20 kills during the Battle of Britain.[5]

THE ATTACK FROM THE NORTH

The skies were clear and sunny on August 15—perfect weather for high-altitude bombing. The Luftwaffe sent bombers based in Norway and Denmark to strike targets in the northern United Kingdom. The bombers had to fly without a fighter escort, since the distance was too great for the limited fuel capacity of the Bf 109s.

Alerted by radar, sector commanders of 13 Group scrambled several fighter squadrons to meet the incoming Heinkels and Junkers. Without German fighters to protect them, the bombers were sitting ducks. Attacking from the flanks, Spitfires and Hurricanes opened fire, dropping several of the lumbering bombers from the sky immediately. Although the German planes managed to land a few bombs on target, most broke formation, turned back, and released their payloads harmlessly into the North Sea.

Even when not facing RAF fighters, German pilots and crews had to navigate through other defenses. Heavy antiaircraft fire and dangerous barrage balloons threatened to destroy their aircraft. The British guns threw up shells that created a black cloud of smoke and sent flying jagged shrapnel that could tear through aircraft skins, shatter glass canopies, and kill crews. At night, the dangers intensified. The clouds of antiaircraft fire were hard to spot on a moonless or cloudy night, and navigation by landmarks on the ground was impossible in the dark.

One German bomber, flying slightly off course, dropped several bombs on Croydon Airfield. Used by the RAF, Croydon represented an important target for the Luftwaffe. But it was located in the London metropolitan area, and Hitler

Large antiaircraft guns made flying hazardous for enemy planes in British skies.

had barred any attack on London. When he heard of the Croydon bombing, he flew into a rage. He knew any attack on London would surely stiffen British resolve. It could also result in retaliation against German cities.

In fact, Croydon would be the first of many London targets to come under attack from the air. Hitler's hesitation to attack civilian areas would come to an end soon. An all-out terror campaign on London and other cities would bring a new and deadlier phase to the Battle of Britain.

Aircraft spotters in London helped track incoming bombers.

BOMBS OVER LONDON

Operation Adlerangriff continued into mid-August, with Luftwaffe bombers arriving in huge formations each day. As the bombers roared overhead at 10,000 feet (3,000 m), civilians on the ground looked up at the sky in fear, and RAF squad and group commanders watched their tabletop maps anxiously. The Luftwaffe fleets were much too large for the smaller British fighter squadrons to stop. Nevertheless, Spitfires and Hurricanes were able to shoot down many bombers. They found the Stuka dive bombers especially easy prey.

As time went on, it became clear to German commanders that Göring could not deliver on his promise to clear the skies over the United Kingdom. In order to get heavy tanks, artillery pieces, and trucks ashore during Operation Sea Lion, the German army would have to capture British ports, including Southampton and Portsmouth. The German navy would have to mine the English

Channel to stop the Royal Navy from interfering. All of these things depended on the Luftwaffe's dominance of the skies.

Hitler postponed the invasion of the United Kingdom once again, this time until September 17. In addition, the Luftwaffe withdrew its Stukas from the skies over the United Kingdom. The dive bombers had terrified civilians in France and Poland, but when faced with fast, well-armed British fighters, they became slow and easy targets.

The pilots of 11 Group flew continuous sorties, and the grueling hours of aerial combat were taking their toll. Dowding ordered the group's pilots and planes to rotate to quieter groups in the north and west of the United Kingdom. Reinforcements arrived in the critical southeast. All the while, the "big wing" controversy continued. Still under pressure to send up larger formations to meet the Germans, Dowding resisted.

NIGHT ATTACKS

The weather in the United Kingdom changes frequently. One day may be fair, the next cold, the next rainy. Clouds and fog are common, even in midsummer. Realizing he could not count on favorable weather, Göring ordered an important change in tactics. The Luftwaffe would start a night bombing campaign.

Normally, night bombing from high altitude is difficult or even impossible. When civilians turn out all the lights in a city, bombing targets become extremely hard to find. Powerful searchlights and antiaircraft guns mean constant danger at high altitude. But the German pilots had a secret weapon at their disposal. The system was known as *Knickebein*, or "crooked leg." It used two radio beacons, spaced far apart, that sent different signals toward a target. Aboard a Luftwaffe

British fighters shot down many German bombers, but reinforcements kept coming over.

bomber, the pilot listened closely to the two signals. As he neared the target, the signals became closer together. When the signals finally converged, he heard a single tone. This meant he was over the target and could drop his payload.

By day, bombers and fighters from Luftflotte 2, or Air Fleet 2, continued attacking Fighter Command airfields in southern England. By night, Luftflotte 3 bombers rained destruction on Britain's major ports and industrial centers, including Birmingham, Bristol, Liverpool, Edinburgh, Newcastle, and Portsmouth.

THE MYTH ABOUT CARROTS

During the Battle of Britain, the RAF developed an airborne radar system that improved British pilots' performance against the Luftwaffe. In addition, Hurricanes and Spitfires used red lights, which do not interfere with night vision, to illuminate their cockpits. To mask these advantages, the RAF created a deception that persists to the present day. The RAF announced its pilots ate carrots every night because the orange vegetable was good for its pilots' night vision. As a result, the myth that carrots improve eyesight has survived, decades after the Battle of Britain.

The RAF was unable to prevent or slow these attacks. Without onboard radar systems, British pilots could find enemy planes only by sight—a task nearly impossible at night. The British Air Ministry was working on an Airborne Interception (AI) system, which would place radar units onboard the fighters. But even when it was ready, the AI system would fit inside only the larger, twin-engine Bristol Blenheims. Spitfires and Hurricanes, which made up the majority of the fighter fleet, were single-engine planes too small to use the new system.

Ground forces used searchlights to locate enemy bombers at night.

AN ATTACK ON LONDON

On the night of August 24, a small squadron of Luftwaffe bombers flying at night missed an important landmark and flew slightly off course. Unable to spot their assigned target, an oil storage facility in Thameshaven, they found themselves above a heavily populated area. Running low on fuel, the pilots dropped their bombs and headed back across the English Channel.

Germany had made its first direct hits on the center of London. When Göring heard the report, he was furious. Göring had reserved for himself the decision to begin the bombing of London. Now that decision was out of his hands.

Angered by the bombing of an area with no military value, Churchill ordered an immediate retaliation on the city of Berlin, the German capital. A squadron of long-range RAF bombers took off every night for the next four nights. For the first time during the war, the people of Berlin heard the eerie and frightening sound of air-raid sirens. Thousands hid in bomb shelters. Although the British bombs did little serious damage, the raids had an effect on the frightened German civilians.

FROM THE GERMAN SIDE

During World War II, US journalist William L. Shirer worked as a CBS radio correspondent. Working and living in Berlin before the United States entered the war, Shirer had to deal with a strict and sometimes threatening German information ministry that controlled and censored his every line. On September 1, 1940, after the first British air attacks on Berlin, he reported on the mood of German civilians:

The main effect of a week of constant British night bombings has been to spread great disillusionment among the people here and sow doubt in their minds. One said to me, "I'll never believe another thing they say. If they've lied about the raids in the rest of Germany as they have about the ones on Berlin, then it must have been pretty bad there."[1]

Shocked and angered, Hitler promised a painful revenge on the British. At a September 4 speech in Berlin, he declared:

> If the British Air Force drops two, three or four thousand kilos of bombs, then we will now drop 150,000, 180,000, 230,000, 300,000, or 400,000 kilos, or more, in one night. If they declare that they will attack our cities on a large scale, we will erase theirs! We will put a stop to the game of these night pirates, as God is our witness. The hour will come when one or the other of us will crumble, and that one will not be National Socialist Germany. I have already carried through such a struggle once in my life, up to the final consequences, and this then led to the collapse of the enemy who is now still sitting there in England on Europe's last island.[2]

Hitler then ordered an all-out terror bombing campaign against London. Göring readily agreed. At this crucial point in the battle, he did not speak against Hitler's wishes.

Although the Luftwaffe was taking heavy losses, the British were losing pilots and planes as well. Dowding was using up his reserves, and there still seemed to be no letup in the German attacks. If more airfields were damaged, the RAF would be unable to scramble planes in time to prevent further bombing. But suddenly, on the orders of Hitler and Göring, the Luftwaffe's bombers halted their attacks on RAF airfields and shifted their attention to London and other cities. This would prove to be a critical mistake.

CIVILIAN SOLDIERS

The Battle of Britain was not a distant, foreign war to the people of the United Kingdom. Instead, the front lines of the battle were directly overhead. When the Luftwaffe began the bombing campaign against London, the city's streets and neighborhoods became filled with danger, noise, and bloodshed. The battle would claim the lives of nearly 40,000 British civilians, a far greater toll than among the fighter pilots of the RAF.[1]

Yet for most people on the ground, life went on much as usual. Shopkeepers and office clerks went to work each morning. Grocery stores did good business, despite the strict food rationing. Schools were open, and cricket and football teams arrived for their matches.

When German planes approached, air-raid sirens began echoing through neighborhoods. Some people took shelter in the London subway system, known as the Underground. Others simply moved

RATIONS

Before the war, British grocers offered their customers a variety of fresh fruits, vegetables, meat, butter, cheese, and wine. But many of these goods were not produced in the United Kingdom and were imported by ship. Others were needed for the war effort. After German submarines began attacks on merchant shipping, the British government started a rationing program. The first ration books went out in January 1940. Each book held detachable coupons that were good for a week's supply of rationed goods. Early in the war, limits were placed on bacon, butter, and sugar. Later, rationing was extended to many other goods. In a typical week, a person might have the right to buy a single egg, four ounces of margarine, four slices of bacon, two ounces of butter, two ounces of tea, one ounce of cheese, and eight ounces of sugar. The ration books also had points that could be saved for spending on cereal, dried fruit, jam, biscuits, and meat.

to the bottom floor or basement levels of their homes. When they looked into the sky, they spotted thin white contrails from fighters rolling, diving, and turning in battle. It was a strange and silent spectacle, as the planes were usually too high to be heard. The air battle reached the ground only when bombs, bullet casings, men in parachutes, or damaged aircraft fell to earth.

Several years before the start of World War II, British towns and cities began enlisting volunteers for the Local Defense Volunteers, later known as the Home Guard. Men who were not eligible for the armed forces were invited to sign up. Although there were teenagers and younger adults in the Home Guard, many members were well past military age, resulting in the nickname Dad's Army.

Members of the Home Guard wore armbands and saucer-shaped hats made of tin. They trained in village greens and parks, learned to march in formation, and dug trenches as bomb shelters and defensive positions. To prepare for the

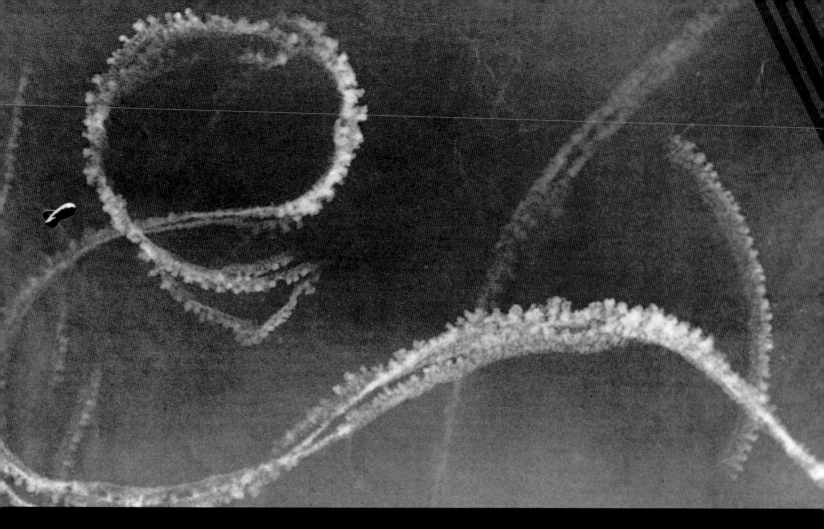

From the ground, white contrails were among the only signs of a battle going on far above.

expected air raids, the volunteers built Air Raid Precaution posts to be manned by observers.

Volunteers also manned outposts of the Royal Observer Corps. By the start of the war, the Observer Corps was running more than 1,000 posts in England,

Scotland, and Wales, using more than 30,000 civilian observers.[2] The posts operated around the clock, seven days a week, throughout the war. Each hut had a telephone, a stove, a pair of binoculars, and a pantograph. This device allowed the observer to measure the height and direction of sighted planes. A telephone call went to the local group control center, which immediately relayed the sighting to the Fighter Command headquarters at Bentley Priory.

BRITAIN'S WARTIME WOMEN

During World War II, the United Kingdom became one of the few nations in history to subject women to a wartime draft. Women were brought into the RAF and civilian organizations as noncombat pilots, control room operators, runners, observers, and factory workers. The increase in factory staff made it possible to greatly increase the output of military aircraft. Meanwhile, the overconfident German government did not bother to run factories more than eight hours a day until 1942. Women there were not recruited as welders, assemblers, or riveters as they were in the United Kingdom and the United States.

FIGHTING WOMEN OF BRITAIN

Women also played an important part in the defense of the United Kingdom, and several civilian organizations accepted them as members. Volunteers for the Women's Auxiliary Air Force (WAAF) worked around large table maps in the ground control centers. Wearing headsets and microphones, they took reports from observer posts and plotted the incoming raids by pushing small tokens across giant maps of the United Kingdom. When a sector commander wanted a unit scrambled into the air, a WAAF member relayed instructions to the pilots, giving them a direction and altitude.

WAAF members also worked as telephone operators, drivers, clerks, and cooks. The radar stations and ground control stations were among the most

Members of the WAAF helped repair and maintain RAF aircraft.

dangerous assignments. Both were prime targets for German dive bombers, and many came under direct attack. Volunteers were expected to stay at their posts despite the threat of a direct hit that might destroy the center and kill everyone working within. Six WAAF members received medals for bravery. Women also crewed antiaircraft guns, operated searchlights, and served as pilots in the Air

Transport Auxiliary service, which delivered planes from factories and repair stations to RAF airfields.

CIVILIANS UNDER FIRE

Foreign observers greatly admired the ability of British civilians to carry on despite the nightly bombing. An important part of the relatively high morale was the sense that the government and the RAF had properly prepared to meet the German threat.

One innovation was known as the Anderson Shelter. This structure was designed to protect up to six people in the backyard of a house. The family raised the frame and covered it with earth. They could then use the shelter when a raid was in progress as protection against bomb fragments and fire. In the months leading up to World War II, the British government distributed 1.5 million Andersons.[3] Many of them were provided free to poor families.

Many British homes did not have yards or cellars. To help protect these people, the inventor John Baker created the Morrison Shelter, which could be assembled inside the home. It was a wire-mesh cage with a

THE ARP SERVICE

One of Europe's largest World War II armies was made up of civilians, not military personnel. The Air Raid Precautions (ARP) force included approximately 1.4 million unpaid British volunteers whose job it was to pass out gas masks, assist families with their portable shelters, and make sure civilians turned lights out at night to prevent enemy bombers from identifying their city.[4] If a house was showing lights at the wrong time, an ARP patrolman or patrolwoman would rap on the door or window of the house and give a strict warning. If a firebomb device fell in the street or on the roof of a house, an ARP member was tasked with putting out the flames before a fire could spread. Volunteers rescued people from bombed-out buildings and helped remove the bodies of the dead.

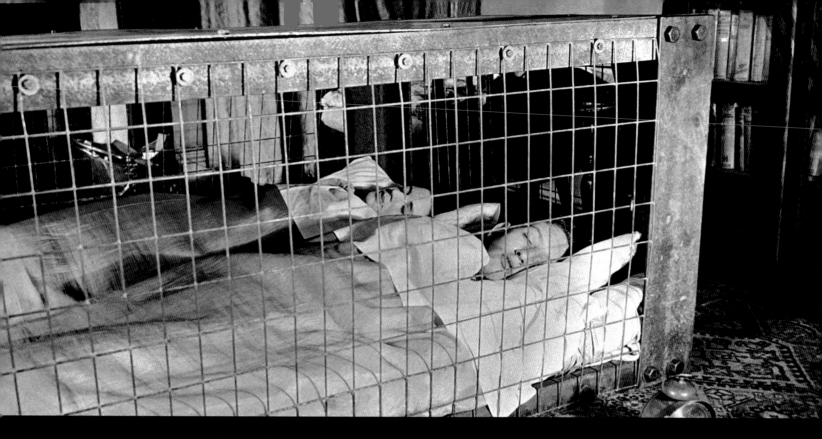

Morrison shelters provided protection for people in Britain's inner cities.

steel plate for a top, measuring approximately six and a half feet (2 m) long by four feet (1.2 m) wide. It was designed to protect the owners from the collapse of the floor above, a common cause of death during air raids. An individual or a family could sleep inside the shelter at night and use it as a table during the day.

Londoners who did not feel safe in their homes also had the option of using Underground stations. City authorities placed bunks, first aid stations, and toilets inside the stations, as well as food and drink services. Shelter marshals were recruited to keep order and direct users to open spots on the platform.

London's tightly packed buildings made German bombing raids highly destructive.

THE BLITZ

The raids on London continued throughout September 1940. The Luftwaffe gradually improved its navigation and radio beacon systems, allowing it to hit targets more accurately at night. But when the target was one of the world's largest cities, and there was no ban on striking civilian houses, exactly what they hit was rarely a concern for German pilots. For two full months, an average of 200 German bombers arrived in the skies over London each night.[1] To citizens of the United Kingdom, the ongoing raids became known as the Blitz.

Antiaircraft crews manned dozens of guns in London. By the time the bomber fleets reached the city, the RAF's radar system was of little help in pinpointing individual planes. At night, the antiaircraft guns—which were not equipped with their own radar systems—had problems getting a clear fix on their targets.

RAF commanders attempted to turn back the raids with fighters alone. When that failed, more guns were brought to London from smaller cities.

THE BLAST AT 10 DOWNING STREET

The Luftwaffe concentrated on the docks along the Thames River, oil storage facilities, factories, warehouses, and densely populated city neighborhoods. Other high-priority targets were the Houses of Parliament and other government buildings, including the prime minister's residence at 10 Downing Street.

UNWILLING GERMAN GUESTS

Downed Luftwaffe pilots who survived were taken captive by local civilians, who were constantly on the lookout for crashing planes and descending parachutes. The prisoners were interned in British camps, and many were shipped off to Canada or the United States. By the end of the war, the prisoner of war population in the United States reached more than 400,000.[2] Camps were set up in every state except Nevada, North Dakota, and Vermont. Many of these camps remained intact after the war, serving as state park shelters, military barracks, historical sites, and recreational centers.

October 17 began as another ordinary day during the Blitz. Air-raid sirens were heard throughout the afternoon and into the evening. Churchill invited several friends to dinner at the Downing Street residence, where maids, butlers, and cooks worked in the back kitchen, enjoying a view of the garden through a tall plate glass window.

A raid began, and the sound of exploding bombs was heard. Accustomed to the noise, the Downing Street staff carried on, preparing the evening meal. Suddenly, on a hunch, Churchill walked from the dining room to the kitchen. He asked for the meal to be set out immediately on hot plates, and ordered the staff into the basement shelter.

Churchill returned to his place. Within minutes, a bomb screamed out of the sky and scored a direct hit on a neighboring government building. The explosion occurred just behind 10 Downing Street. The prime minister described the scene:

> *I had been seated again at table only about three minutes when a really very loud crash, close at hand, and a violent shock showed that the house had been struck. . . . We went into the kitchen to view the scene. The devastation was complete. The bomb had fallen fifty yards [46 m] away on the Treasury, and the blast had smitten the large, tidy kitchen, with all its bright saucepans and crockery, into a heap of black dust and rubble.*[3]

Churchill narrowly escaped death when bombs fell near his home in London.

Edward R. Murrow and other journalists based in London provided the United States with updates on the bombing of the United Kingdom.

Despite the constant danger, Churchill remained in London throughout the Blitz. He often traveled to neighborhoods hard hit by the previous night's bombing. Londoners instantly recognized the prime minister and pressed forward to meet him, shake his hand, and offer words of encouragement. Instead of allowing fear to overcome them and drive them away from their homes and jobs, Londoners grew increasingly defiant.

Inspired by the stubborn resistance of ordinary people, Churchill proposed an important measure to the British government. Using public funds, the Treasury department would set up an insurance pool. Anyone with a home or shop damaged in the bombing could file a claim for damages. The insurance applied to every citizen. It would pay for any damage caused by hostile enemy action.

BOMB DAMAGE

In September, the Luftwaffe began using new weapons against London, including incendiary bombs designed to ignite and spread damaging fires. When incendiary bombs fell on a city block, if wind conditions were right the separate fires would quickly join into one larger fire that would be very difficult to stop.

To deal with incendiary bombs, the city passed the Fire Watchers Order. This law compelled all businesses to have someone watching for fires and explosives at all times. Volunteer fire watchers observed surrounding neighborhoods from tall rooftops. With portable telephones at hand, they immediately reported any fires that broke out to a central dispatch station, which then sent firefighters to douse the flames. These fire watchers were in much greater danger than observers in the countryside; they wore only tin hats for protection against bombs and shrapnel.

"THIS IS LONDON"

Every evening during the Battle of Britain, CBS Radio reporter Edward R. Murrow reported from London, always beginning his reports with the phrase "This is London." The city was under daily attack by the Luftwaffe, yet Murrow remained at his post, climbing rooftops to get a better view and taking shelter only when absolutely necessary. In his broadcast of September 10, 1940, he reported on one of the Luftwaffe's first incendiary attacks on London:

> We could see little men shoveling those fire bombs into the river. One burned for a few minutes like a beacon right in the middle of a bridge. Finally those white flames all went out. No one bothers about the white light, it's only when it turns yellow that a real fire has started. I must have seen well over a hundred fire bombs come down and only three small fires were started. The incendiaries aren't so bad if there is someone there to deal with them, but those oil bombs present more difficulties. As I watched those white fires flame up and die down, watched the yellow blazes grow dull and disappear, I thought, what a puny effort is this to burn a great city.[4]

To disrupt road and rail traffic, the Germans also used delayed action bombs, which crashed to the ground without detonating. The fuses on these devices remained live even if the bombs burrowed deep into the ground. The surrounding area had to be blocked off so bomb disposal squads could defuse the bomb. The ground and debris around the bomb had to be cleared away. Then, the fuse housed in the nose of the bomb had to be opened and deactivated. If that did not work, the bombs had to be safely detonated by remote control. Any error could be fatal. It was dangerous work that claimed many civilian lives.

By the first week of November, London had been under daily bombing for almost two months. There seemed no end in sight to the nightly assault from

Firefighters worked quickly to put out blazes started by incendiary bombs.

the air. Entire neighborhoods now lay in smoking ruin, and life in the city was growing more unpleasant. Even basic city services were under threat. In October, the Germans had scored a direct hit on London's sewer system, forcing the city to dump raw sewage into the Thames River.

On November 3, Göring made another change in Luftwaffe strategy. The German bombers would continue the city bombing campaign, but instead of London they would fly against other targets: major industrial centers, such as Liverpool and Birmingham. The shift meant the end of the Blitz. The harshest period of the Battle of Britain was over. Hitler again delayed Operation Sea Lion, putting it off until the spring.

On November 14, a fleet of German bombers unleashed a devastating attack on Coventry, pulverizing the center of the city. The attack killed 600 people, yet it left the largest factories in the city with only minor damage.[5] Meanwhile, Londoners scrambled to repair damaged buildings and restore services. The lull in the bombing gave the city several much-needed days of quiet, giving observers, firefighters, and shelter marshals a chance to rest. Once again, German leaders had made a mistake by switching targets. London came under occasional bombing only until the spring of 1941, when Hitler would shift his attention to a much larger target: the Soviet Union.

The attack on Coventry destroyed the city's historic cathedral and many other buildings.

Observation aircraft captured images of the planned Sea Lion invasion fleet in French ports.

HARD-FOUGHT VICTORY

After Operation Sea Lion was delayed until the spring of 1941, German commanders dispersed the landing barges and equipment they had assembled at the French ports of Dunkirk and Cherbourg. The armies preparing for the invasion transferred to eastern Europe and prepared for an invasion of the Soviet Union.

However, the Luftwaffe was not done with the British. Bombings of London and other cities continued through the winter of 1940 to 1941. But Göring could no longer send fleets of more than 1,000 planes across the English Channel in massive daytime assaults. The RAF, the Fighter Command radar and ground control system, the searchlights and barrage balloons, and the army of civilian observers had denied Germany command of the skies.

The RAF, growing more confident that Germany could not mount an invasion, began sending more aircraft on missions across the English Channel to German-occupied France. They attacked the

German military bases and strategic rail junctions allowing the German army to move its units quickly across France.

RAF pilots found the skies over France much more difficult than those over their homeland. While German pilots could return to the fighting if they were shot down and survived, downed British pilots now ran the risk of being taken prisoner. Flying far from their bases, they had no opportunity to refuel and return to the air. There was also no ground control to steer them toward enemy formations.

Although their aerial combat was deadly, British and German pilots still showed mutual respect for their courage and skill. As in World War I, fighter pilots on both sides often showed a sense of honor and fair play that extended to enemy pilots taken prisoner.

In August 1941, RAF pilot Douglas Bader, who had lost both of his legs in a prewar accident, was shot down over France while dogfighting in a Spitfire. He barely escaped from the plane as it spiraled toward the ground, losing one of his prosthetic legs. The Luftwaffe permitted the RAF to drop a replacement leg for their captured ace. Widely admired among German pilots, Bader was given a dinner personally by Luftwaffe ace Adolf Galland before being shipped off to a prisoner of war camp at Colditz Castle in Germany, where he spent the rest of the war.

HITLER TURNS EAST

As the bombing of London continued, RAF attacks on Germany intensified. The heavy bombing of the port city of Lübeck in March 1942 brought a German reprisal. Hitler ordered the Luftwaffe to again concentrate on civilian targets in

ADOLF GALLAND

1912–1996

Born in the German province of Westphalia, Adolf Galland began building model planes at age 12 and piloting gliders at age 16. A gifted pilot, he earned his commercial flying license, took a job at an airline, and was recruited into the secret air force Germany began building after Hitler came to power.

The Spanish Civil War (1936–1939) served as an early training ground for Luftwaffe bomber and fighter pilots. Germany sent aircraft to support one side of the conflict. Galland gained experience on these missions. With the outbreak of World War II, he flew fighter missions in Poland before transferring to the Battle of Britain, where he shot down two British planes during his first mission. By the end of the war he had collected an incredible total of 104 victories—more than any other pilot on either side of the conflict.

As the war continued, however, Galland grew unhappy with Hitler's leadership. He later described his feelings in an interview:

I was not very impressed with him. The first time I met him was after Spain when we were summoned to the Reichschancellery. There was Hitler, short, gray-faced and not very strong, and he spoke with a crisp language. He did not allow us to smoke, nor did he offer us anything to drink, nothing like that. This impression was strengthened every year I knew him as his mistakes mounted and cost German lives, the mistakes that Göring should have brought to his attention.[1]

the United Kingdom. The RAF then began striking industrial cities in western Germany, including Cologne, Essen, Düsseldorf, Hamburg, and Dortmund. The goal was to demoralize German civilians and knock out Germany's ability to produce tanks, ships, artillery, vehicles, and aircraft.

As the war continued, and the Luftwaffe continued losing aircraft and pilots, poor German intelligence hindered the effort to subdue the RAF. The head of Luftwaffe intelligence, Joseph Schmid, tailored his reports to suit Göring's false opinion of British weakness and German superiority. Schmid constantly underestimated the RAF's fighter strength and overestimated the damage being done by the bombing runs over London and other British cities. Luftwaffe pilots and officers distrusted him because he had never been a pilot himself. They believed he did not understand his own reports on enemy strength and positioning.

In the end, Germany never attempted an invasion of the United Kingdom. Instead, in June 1941, Hitler ordered his armies to invade the Soviet Union. Hundreds of German divisions crossed Germany's eastern frontier. Panzer tanks easily smashed through the Soviet defenses, and the Luftwaffe destroyed

CRACKING THE CODE

During the Battle of Britain, the RAF benefited from one of the most important victories of the war: the cracking of Enigma, the coded language used by the German military for its messages and orders. A team of code breakers assembled at Bletchley Park, a country mansion in Buckinghamshire, to work on Enigma and other codes before the war. Their achievement allowed Dowding and Fighter Command to get a much clearer picture of German strategy during the battle, including the strength and location of Luftwaffe squadrons in northern France and advance warning of large-scale attacks planned by the enemy.

RAF pilots and crews celebrated after successfully bombing Cologne, Germany.

much of the Soviet air force on the ground before it could even put up a defense. The Soviet army retreated east.

In December 1941, Japan attacked the US naval and air bases at Pearl Harbor, Hawaii. Bombs and torpedoes sunk several major warships and destroyed dozens of planes parked on the ground. On the day following the attack, the United States declared war on Japan. Standing with its ally, Germany declared war on the United States.

In Churchill's "We Shall Never Surrender" speech, he had predicted "the New World, with all its power and might," would "[step] forth to the rescue and the liberation of the old."[2] With the United States now involved in the war on the side of the United Kingdom, he was proved correct.

THE TURNING POINT

The Battle of Britain proved to be a crucial turning point in World War II. For several months in the summer of 1940, the British stood alone against Nazi domination of Europe. Churchill's stubborn refusal to negotiate with Hitler kept the Luftwaffe deployed in northern Europe, where it proved unable to deliver the knockout blow to the RAF.

In the spring of 1944, a massive Allied army gathered in southern England. American, Canadian, and British soldiers trained for battle. Their commander, US General Dwight Eisenhower, would soon lead an invasion of German-occupied France across the English Channel. Originally, Eisenhower planned to launch the invasion in May. Bad weather delayed the actual invasion until June 6. On this day—known as D-Day—the Allies returned to Europe.

Barrage balloons protected the D-Day invasion fleet from counterattacks by

The German defenders were thrown back from the coast and gradually retreated across northern France. Soon afterward, Germany also began deploying a new weapon called the V-1. This was an unpiloted, self-propelled, winged bomb powered by a jet engine. The *V* stood for *Vergeltungswaffe*, or "vengeance weapon." It was intended to pay the British back for their raids on German cities. For the peculiar noise it made while in the air, the British called the V-1 the buzz bomb.

Starting in June 1944, the Germans launched 10,000 buzz bombs at targets in the United Kingdom.[3] Once again, the Observer Corps was called to duty, and the shelters of London filled with nervous citizens. A second Battle of Britain had begun. Fortunately for the British, many V-1s were shot down by RAF fighters or flew off course to land harmlessly in the English Channel. Antiaircraft guns were equipped with proximity fuses, devices within the shells that detonated them as soon as they got near a target. These proved effective in combating the V-1 threat. The Allied forces pouring across northern France eventually managed to overrun many of the launch sites.

The Germans also employed an even deadlier weapon: the V-2, a liquid-fueled rocket bomb that was launched many miles into the atmosphere and then fell back to Earth faster than the speed of sound. This made it extremely difficult to track. People on the ground were unable to hear the bombs coming, leaving them unable to take shelter in time to avoid the massive detonation.

Approximately 1,100 V-2s reached London.[4] The Germans also launched them against Antwerp, Belgium, where many of the military supplies and reinforcements arrived for the Allied armies now marching toward Germany.

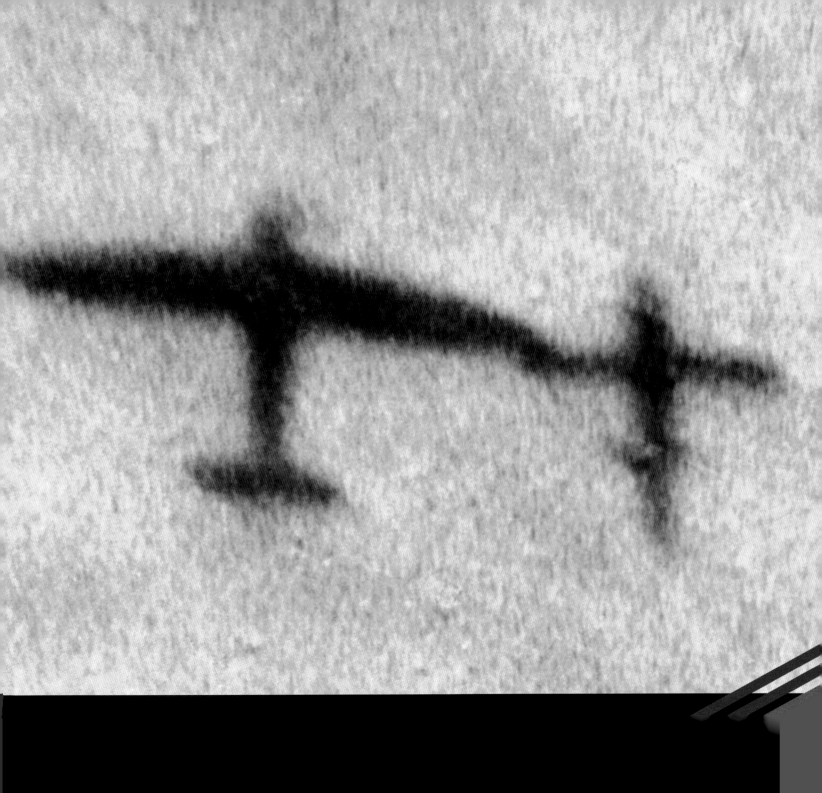

The V-2 did little damage to important military or strategic targets, but it was a terrifying weapon for civilians on the ground. After the war, the V-2 became the model for modern rocket weapons.

THE WAR'S END

In the spring of 1945, the V-2 bases were overrun along with the rest of Germany. A devastating bombing campaign destroyed vast swaths of German cities, including Dresden, Hamburg, and Berlin. The Allied armies drove into Berlin, where Adolf Hitler committed suicide on April 30. Germany surrendered on May 7. Japan held out until the United States dropped atomic bombs on the cities of Hiroshima and Nagasaki in August. Japan finally surrendered.

The Battle of Britain represented a turning point in the history of warfare. For the first time, air-to-air combat played a key role in individual battles, and dominance of the skies decided the war's winners and losers. Without air superiority, invasions and major offensives are difficult, no matter how well prepared ground forces are. In addition, the air war brought civilians into the line of fire. Cities

THE BETHNAL GREEN TUBE DISASTER

Although the German bombing campaign over London slowed after May 1941, Londoners still took casualties. One of the worst incidents took place when there was no bombing at all. On March 3, 1943, air-raid sirens sounded over London. When an antiaircraft battery opened fire, a panic spread among a large crowd trying to get into the Bethnal Green Underground station in the East End. A woman holding a child fell on the steps leading down to the station, and hundreds of people behind her also began tumbling forward. The massive crush killed 173 people from injuries and suffocation.[5]

The Allies captured and studied V-2 rockets after Germany's surrender.

Churchill's steadfast refusal to surrender helped inspire the British to withstand devastating bomber attacks.

such as London and Berlin came under attack even when located hundreds or thousands of miles from the front lines.

The battle also proved civilians can play crucial roles in winning a war. The resolve of the British people to carry on their normal lives despite the daily threat of death and destruction helped the United Kingdom hold out through months of brutal attacks. Eventually, their determination prevented the invasion of their country and led to their victory over Nazi Germany.

TIMELINE

1933

Germany secretly establishes its new Luftwaffe, or air force.

1936

The Royal Air Force (RAF) creates Fighter Command, under the leadership of Hugh Dowding.

1936

Production of Supermarine Spitfires and Hawker Hurricanes begins in the United Kingdom.

September 1, 1939

Germany invades Poland, starting World War II.

August 13, 1940

The Luftwaffe launches a massive air attack code-named *Adlerangriff,* or "Eagle Attack."

August 24, 1940

A group of off-course Luftwaffe bombers release their bombs over London.

September 1940

The Luftwaffe begins a devastating two-month aerial bombing campaign against London.

October 17, 1940

A bomb falls near the prime minister's residence at 10 Downing Street in London.

July 16, 1940

Adolf Hitler begins preparations for Operation Sea Lion, the invasion of the United Kingdom.

July 3, 1940

Winston Churchill instructs the Royal Navy to demand the surrender of French ships in Algeria.

June 1940

Hermann Göring orders Luftwaffe attacks on RAF airfields and radar installations in southern England.

Late May, 1940

The British Expeditionary Force begins a mass evacuation from the port of Dunkirk in France.

November 3, 1940

Göring shifts the Luftwaffe bombing attacks away from London to other British cities.

June 1941

Germany transfers Luftwaffe bombers and fighters to the eastern front.

June 1944

Germany begins launching V-1 bombs against London.

May 7, 1945

Germany surrenders, bringing World War II to a close in Europe.

ESSENTIAL FACTS

KEY PLAYERS

- Adolf Hitler: Leader of the Nazi Party and the German government from 1933 to 1945.

- Hermann Göring: Commander of the Luftwaffe, the air force of Nazi Germany.

- Hugh Dowding: Commander of RAF Fighter Command during the Battle of Britain.

- Winston Churchill: Prime minister of the United Kingdom during the Battle of Britain.

KEY STATISTICS

AIRCRAFT DEPLOYED

- Germany: 1,223 fighters, 1,482 bombers, 327 dive bombers

- Britain: 903 fighters, 560 bombers, 500 coastal aircraft

CREW LOSSES

- Germany 2,662; United Kingdom 537

- Civilian death toll: 43,000

KEY AIRCRAFT

- Heinkel He 111: The He 111 was a heavy German bomber that was one of the principal Luftwaffe weapons used during the Battle of Britain.

- Hawker Hurricane: The Hurricane was a fast and maneuverable British fighter used effectively against German bombers.

- Supermarine Spitfire: The Spitfire was a fast, well-armed single-engine RAF fighter used effectively against German bombers and fighters.

IMPACT ON THE WAR

By tying up the Luftwaffe for several months in the summer of 1940, the RAF depleted German air power, lessened the ranks of experienced Luftwaffe pilots, and stopped the planned invasion of Britain. This degraded Germany's ability to mount further offensives on the European continent as well as its ability to defend itself from bombing attacks on German cities that would intensify later in the war. Britain's refusal to surrender or to reach a peace agreement with Germany prevented total domination of western Europe by Germany in 1940.

QUOTE

"We shall go on to the end, we shall fight in France, we shall fight on the seas and oceans, we shall fight with growing confidence and growing strength in the air, we shall defend our island, whatever the cost may be, we shall fight on the beaches, we shall fight on the landing grounds, we shall fight in the fields and in the streets, we shall fight in the hills; we shall never surrender."

—*Winston Churchill*

GLOSSARY

CONTRAIL

A thin cloud that forms behind an aircraft, caused by engine exhaust or the movement of air over the wings.

DIVISION

A large, self-contained military unit typically made up of 15,000 to 20,000 troops.

DOGFIGHT

An aerial battle between single opposing planes or groups of planes.

EXPEDITIONARY

Traveling to another place.

PROPAGANDA

Information that carries facts or details slanted to favor a single point of view or political bias.

RADAR

A technology that involves bouncing radio waves off of distant objects to determine their location, size, and speed.

SCRAMBLE

To rapidly get into one's fighter plane and take off to combat an immediate threat.

SHRAPNEL

Small metal fragments that are flung into the air by an exploding shell or bomb, causing risk of injury or death to anyone nearby.

SORTIE

A mission by a single unit, such as a plane, against enemy forces. For military fliers, a sortie is a flight intended to meet enemy aircraft or to carry out bombing of an enemy target.

SQUADRON

A group of aircraft making up a single unit within an air force.

ADDITIONAL RESOURCES

SELECTED BIBLIOGRAPHY

Holland, James. *The Battle of Britain: Five Months that Changed History.* New York: Saint Martin's, 2010. Print.

Korda, Michael. *With Wings Like Eagles: A History of the Battle of Britain.* New York: Harper, 2009. Print.

FURTHER READINGS

Graham, Ian. *You Wouldn't Want to Be A World War II Pilot: Air Battles You Might Not Survive.* New York: Scholastic, 2009. Print.

Priestly, Chris. *My Story: Battle of Britain.* New York: Scholastic, 2012. Print.

WEBSITES

To learn more about Essential Library of World War II, visit **booklinks.abdopublishing.com**. These links are routinely monitored and updated to provide the most current information available.

Royal Air Force Museum
Grahame Park Way
London, NW9 5LL
United Kingdom
+44 020-8358-4964
http://www.rafmuseum.org.uk
This museum features aircraft from throughout the history of the RAF, including many of the major British and German fighters of the Battle of Britain.

Spitfire and Hurricane Memorial Museum
The Airfield, Ramston Road
Ramsgate, Kent CT12 5DF
United Kingdom
+44 1843-821940
http://www.spitfiremuseum.org.uk
This museum is dedicated to the two top RAF fighters of the Battle of Britain.

SOURCE NOTES

CHAPTER 1. MIDAIR DUELS

1. "The Airmen's Stories." *The Battle of Britain London Monument*. Battle of Britain Archive, 2007. Web. 23 Mar. 2015.

2. Huw Jones. "601 Squadron: Millionaire Flying Aces of World War II." *BBC News*. BBC, 14 Dec. 2010. Web. 23 Mar. 2015.

3. "Spitfire and Hurricane." *Royal Air Force*. Royal Air Force, 2015. Web. 23 Mar. 2015.

4. "Eagle Squadrons." *Royal Air Force Museum*. Royal Air Force Museum, 2013. Web. 23 Mar. 2015.

5. "Who Were the Few." *Royal Air Force*. Royal Air Force, 2015. Web. 23 Mar. 2015.

6. Adam Edwards. "The Heroic Flying Toffs." *Express*. Northern and Shell Media Publications, 18 Dec. 2010. Web. 23 Mar. 2015.

7. "Battle of Britain." *Royal Air Force Museum*. Royal Air Force Museum, 2013. Web. 23 Mar. 2015.

CHAPTER 2. THE PHONY WAR AND DUNKIRK

1. "Invasion of Poland." *Holocaust Encyclopedia*. United States Holocaust Museum, 20 June 2014. Web. 23 Mar. 2015.

2. "Treaty of Versailles, 1919." *Holocaust Encyclopedia*. United States Holocaust Museum, 20 June 2014. Web. 23 Mar. 2015.

3. Denis Richards. "Coastal and Fighter Commands." *Royal Air Force 1939–1945*. HyperWar, n.d. Web. 23 Mar. 2015.

4. Ellen Castelow. "Evacuation of Dunkirk." *Historic UK*. Historic UK, 2015. Web. 23 Mar. 2015.

CHAPTER 3. THEIR FINEST HOUR

1. Michael Korda. *With Wings Like Eagles: A History of the Battle of Britain*. New York: Harper, 2009. Print. 134.

2. Winston Churchill. "We Shall Fight on the Beaches." *Churchill Centre*. Churchill Centre, 2015. Web. 23 Mar. 2015.

3. James Holland. *The Battle of Britain: Five Months That Changed History*. New York: Saint Martin's, 2010. Print. 332–333.

CHAPTER 4. EAGLE ATTACK

1. James Holland. *The Battle of Britain: Five Months That Changed History*. New York: Saint Martin's, 2010. Print. 431.

2. "Interview with World War II *Luftwaffe* Ace Günther Rall." *HistoryNet*. HistoryNet, 12 June 2006. Web. 23 Mar. 2015.

3. Richard Hough and Denis Richards. *The Battle of Britain: The Greatest Air Battle of World War II*. New York: Norton, 2005. Print. 145.

4. "Germany Bombs London." *BBC History*. BBC, 2015. Web. 23 Mar. 2015.

5. Alfred Price. *Spitfire Mark I/II Aces 1939-41*. Oxford, UK: Osprey, 1996. Web. 23 Mar. 2015.

SOURCE NOTES
CONTINUED

CHAPTER 5. BOMBS OVER LONDON

1. William Shirer. *Berlin Diary*. Baltimore, MD: Johns Hopkins U, 2002. Print. 493–494.

2. "Wednesday, September 4." *The Battle of Britain 1940*. Battle of Britain Historical Society, 2007. Web. 24 Mar. 2015.

CHAPTER 6. CIVILIAN SOLDIERS

1. "The Battle of Britain." *Royal Air Force*. Royal Air Force, 2015. Web. 23 Mar. 2015.

2. James Holland. *The Battle of Britain: Five Months That Changed History*. New York: Saint Martin's, 2010. Print. 347.

3. "Air Raid Shelter Protection." *Royal Air Force Museum*. Royal Air Force Museum, 2013. Web. 23 Mar. 2015.

4. Ibid.

CHAPTER 7. THE BLITZ

1. Alan Axelrod. *Encyclopedia of World War II, Volume 1*. New York: Facts on File, 2007. Print. 188.

2. J. Malcolm Garcia. "German POWs on the American Homefront." *Smithsonian Magazine*. Smithsonian, 15 Sept. 2009. Web. 24 Mar. 2015.

3. Winston Churchill. *Their Finest Hour*. New York: Mariner, 1986. Print. 306.

4. C. L. Sulzberger. *American Heritage Picture History of World War II*. New York: American Heritage, 1966. Print. 112–115.

5. Marc Ambinder. "History Detective: Did Churchill Sacrifice a City to Protect a Secret?" *The Week*. The Week, 5 Dec. 2012. Web. 24 Mar. 2015.

CHAPTER 8. HARD-FOUGHT VICTORY

1. "Interview with World War II *Luftwaffe* General and Ace Pilot Adolf Galland." *HistoryNet*. HistoryNet, 12 June 2006. Web. 23 Mar. 2015.

2. Winston Churchill. "We Shall Fight on the Beaches." *Churchill Centre*. Churchill Centre, 2015. Web. 23 Mar. 2015.

3. Louise Wilmot. "Germany's Final Measures in World War II." *BBC History*. BBC, 17 Feb. 2011. Web. 24 Mar. 2015.

4. "German Rocketry." *New Mexico State University*. New Mexico State University, 2015. Web. 24 Mar. 2015.

5. Simon B. "The Bethnal Green Tube Shelter Disaster." *WW2 People's War*. BBC, 29 July 2002. Web. 24 Mar. 2015.

INDEX

ABOUT THE AUTHOR

Tom Streissguth has worked as a journalist, teacher, law clerk, courier, and book editor, and he has published more than 100 works of nonfiction. A graduate of Yale University, he is the founder of The Archive, an independent publisher of historical journalism collections used by teachers, students, and researchers. He currently lives in Woodbury, Minnesota.